Beloved

A LOVE LETTER FROM GOD

TONYA KAY MCKINLEY

AT THE WELL PRESS

Contents

To every heart that has picked up this book, thank you. Your journey matters, your story is precious, and I am honored to share these words with you. To my family, friends, and faith community who continually encourage and inspire me—thank you for your unwavering support and prayers. Most importantly, all glory and gratitude to my Heavenly Father, whose love is the heartbeat of every word written here.

Introduction

Beloved,

Before you turn another page, pause for a moment. Breathe. This book is not just ink on paper; it is a reflection of My heart, written just for you. I see you. I know you. I have been with you through every moment—the ones you celebrate and the ones you wish you could forget. Nothing about you is hidden from Me, yet nothing about you has ever made Me turn away.

I want you to know something that could change everything: You are loved. Not with a fleeting, fragile kind of love, but with a love that is eternal, unshakable, and fierce. My love for you is not based on what you have done or left undone. It is not diminished by your mistakes or brokenness. It is not earned, and it cannot be lost. It simply is because I am.

I have watched over you with the tenderness of a Father, the devotion of a Friend, and the passion of the One who created you with purpose and intention. You are not an accident. You are not forgotten. You are not beyond the reach of grace.

Throughout these pages, you will find whispers of My heart woven into every word. Words to remind you that you are cherished beyond measure, pursued with relentless love, and held in the palm of My hand. No matter your past, no matter the scars you carry, I long to heal your heart, to restore what has been broken, and to breathe life into the dreams you thought were lost.

So, come as you are. Bring your doubts, your fears, your weariness. There is no need to pretend here. My love has already made room for you.

With all My heart,

Your Heavenly Father

You Are Loved

Beloved,

From the moment I formed you in the secret place, My love for you has been unchanging and unwavering. Before you spoke your first word, before you took your first step, I loved you. Not because of anything you did or could ever do, but simply because you are Mine.

My love is not like human love, fragile and fickle. It does not fade with time or change with circumstances. My love is eternal—the same yesterday, today, and forever. I declared My love for you through the beauty of creation, through the words written in My Word, and ultimately, through the sacrifice of My Son, Jesus.

Do you know how valuable you are to Me? You are more precious than the finest jewels, more treasured than the rarest of treasures. I have carved your name on the palms of My hands (Isaiah 49:16). I count every hair on your head (Luke 12:7), and My thoughts about you outnumber the grains of sand (Psalm 139:17-18).

When you feel unworthy, remember this: My love does not depend on your worthiness; it defines it. You are worthy because I have called you worthy. You are beloved because I have set My heart upon you. There is nothing you can do to make Me love you more, and nothing you have done can make Me love you less.

Even in your darkest moments, I was there. My heart ached with yours, and My arms were always open, waiting for you to lean into Me. You were never alone, even when you felt abandoned. My love was, is, and always will be the constant in your life, a light that never goes out.

Let these words sink deep into your heart: *You are loved.* Not for what you can offer, not for what you achieve, but simply because you are My beloved child.

With an everlasting love,

Your Heavenly Father

"I have loved you with an everlasting love; I have drawn you with unfailing kindness."

JEREMIAH 31:3

Cherished Beyond Measure

Beloved,

Do you know how precious you are to Me? You are not just seen; you are cherished. Not with a distant, casual affection, but with a love so deep, so intimate, that it surpasses human understanding. My heart delights in you. Yes, *you*.

When I created the heavens and the earth, I spoke them into existence. But when I created you, I formed you with My own hands, breathing My very breath into your being (Genesis 2:7). You are not a mere creation; you are a masterpiece, crafted with care and intention, woven together in your mother's womb (Psalm 139:13-14).

You are not just loved; you are treasured. Imagine the most valuable gem, hidden deep within the earth, guarded and protected because of its worth. That is how I see you. But unlike a gem that can be lost or stolen, your value in My eyes is secure, eternal, and unchanging.

When you feel overlooked or forgotten, remember this: I have engraved you on the palms of My hands (Isaiah 49:16). Every detail of your life matters to Me—your hopes, your fears, your silent prayers whispered in the dark. I bottle every tear you shed (Psalm 56:8), and My thoughts about you are more numerous than the grains of sand (Psalm 139:17-18).

You are the apple of My eye (Zechariah 2:8), the one I sing over with joy (Zephaniah 3:17). When you laugh, My heart rejoices. When you cry, My heart aches with you.

There is no part of your life too small or too messy for Me to care about.

I cherish you not because of what you do, but because of who you are. You are My beloved, My delight, My treasure. My love for you is not fragile; it is fierce and unyielding. It does not waver with time or circumstance. You are held, not by your strength, but by the strength of My everlasting arms (Deuteronomy 33:27).

So, hold this truth close: You are cherished beyond measure, beyond comprehension, beyond anything this world could ever offer. Nothing can diminish your worth in My eyes.

With endless affection,

Your Heavenly Father

"See, I have engraved you on the palms of My hands; your walls are ever before Me."

ISAIAH 49:16

Pursued by Grace

Beloved,

Have you ever felt like you were running? Maybe not with your feet, but with your heart—running from mistakes, from pain, from the places where you feel you fall short. But even as you run, there is Someone who has never stopped pursuing you. That Someone is Me.

I am the God who pursues. I do not wait for you to find Me; I come after you with a love that refuses to give up. My grace is not passive; it is active, reaching out to you in the deepest, most hidden places of your heart.

Remember the story of the prodigal son (Luke 15:11-32)? The son believed he had gone too far, made too many mistakes. But what did his father do? He ran to meet him, arms wide open, heart full of compassion. That is My heart for you. When you turn toward Me, even slightly, I run to you with joy, eager to wrap you in My love.

And think of the woman at the well (John 4). She thought she was just going to get water, trying to avoid the judgmental glances of others. But I had an appointment with her heart. I saw her, knew her story, and still offered her living water—not because she had her life together, but because she needed My grace. I pursue you the same way, not because of what you have done, but because of who you are to Me.

You may believe you are too broken, too distant, too lost. But hear this: There is no distance I will not cross, no barrier I will not break, to reach you. My love crosses deserts, climbs mountains, and walks through the darkest valleys to find you.

You do not have to strive to be worthy of My pursuit. I pursue you because My love is relentless, and My grace is greater than your fears, failures, or flaws. You cannot outrun Me because My love moves faster than your doubt.

So stop running, beloved. Let Me catch you. Let My grace cover you, heal you, and hold you. I have never stopped pursuing you, and I never will.

With relentless love,

Your Heavenly Father

"Surely Your goodness and unfailing love will pursue me all the days of my life, and I will live in the house of the Lord forever."

PSALM 23:6

Your Past Does Not Define You

Beloved,

I know your story—every chapter, every line, even the parts you wish you could erase. But here is a truth I want you to hold tightly: *Your past does not define you.* Your mistakes, your regrets, your pain—they do not have the final say over who you are or who you are becoming.

When I look at you, I do not see your failures. I see My beloved child, washed in grace, clothed in righteousness, and filled with purpose. I do not define you by what you have done or what has been done to you. I define you by what I have done for you.

Through My Son, Jesus, I have made all things new (2 Corinthians 5:17). The cross was not just an event in history; it was a divine exchange. Your guilt for My grace. Your shame for My glory. Your brokenness for My healing. I did not come to condemn you; I came to redeem you (John 3:17).

Remember Rahab? She was labeled by her past, known as a woman with a reputation. But I saw beyond her history. I saw her faith, her courage, her heart. And I wove her into the lineage of My Son (Matthew 1:5). I can do the same with your story. Your past is not a disqualification; it is a testimony waiting to be redeemed.

Think of Peter, who denied Me three times. In his failure, he thought he had lost his place, but I met him with forgiveness, not condemnation. I restored him, reaffirmed his calling, and used him to build My church (John 21:15-17).

You are not the sum of your mistakes. You are not the lies spoken over you or the wounds you carry. You are Mine. My love covers your past, My grace defines your present, and My purpose shapes your future.

Do not let shame be the author of your story. Let Me rewrite it with the ink of redemption and the pages of new beginnings. You are more than your past. You are a new creation, loved beyond measure, and destined for greatness in Me.

With a heart full of grace,

Your Heavenly Father

"Therefore, if anyone is in Christ, the new creation has come: The old has gone, the new is here!"

2 CORINTHIANS
5:17

Healing for the Brokenhearted

Beloved,

I see the hidden places of your heart—the wounds no one else knows about, the silent tears you have cried in the dark, the pain you have carried for far too long. You do not have to pretend with Me. I am close to the brokenhearted, and I bind up their wounds (Psalm 34:18; Psalm 147:3).

Your heart matters to Me. Every shattered piece, every scar, every bruise left by disappointment, betrayal, loss, or fear—I hold them tenderly. I am not repelled by your brokenness; I am drawn to it because I am the Healer of hearts.

When Jesus walked the earth, He sought out the hurting. The woman with the issue of blood, the blind man crying out for mercy, the leper cast out by society—I stopped for them, not because they were whole, but because they were hurting. I have not changed. I still stop for the brokenhearted. I stop for you.

I know the ache of grief and the sting of rejection. My Son felt it, too. He was despised and rejected, a man of sorrows, acquainted with grief (Isaiah 53:3). There is no pain you feel that I do not understand. And there is no sorrow I cannot heal.

You may wonder, "Can these dry bones live?" (Ezekiel 37:3). Yes, beloved, they can. I am the God who breathes life into what feels dead. I speak hope into despair, light into darkness, and healing into brokenness.

Healing does not mean forgetting or pretending it did not hurt. It means letting Me into those places to restore what was lost, to give beauty for ashes, the oil of joy for mourning, and a garment of praise instead of a spirit of despair (Isaiah 61:3).

You are not beyond repair. You are not too broken for My touch. My hands are gentle, My heart is kind, and My love is strong enough to carry you through the healing process. Let Me in. Let Me hold your heart and whisper truth where lies have taken root.

You are seen. You are heard. You are loved. And healing is yours in Me.

With tender compassion,

Your Heavenly Father

"He heals the brokenhearted and binds up their wounds."

PSALM 147:3

You Have a Destiny

Beloved,

Before you were born, I knew you. Before you took your first breath, I had already written a story for your life—one filled with purpose, hope, and destiny (Jeremiah 29:11). You are not here by accident. Every detail of your existence is woven into the fabric of My divine plan.

You may wonder, *"Do I really matter? Is there a reason for my life?"* Yes, beloved. You matter more than you can imagine. I have placed gifts within you, dreams that reflect the beauty of My design. Your life has a purpose that no one else can fulfill because you are uniquely created by My hand (Ephesians 2:10).

Destiny is not about perfection. It is about walking with Me, step by step, even when the path is unclear. Think of Moses, who doubted his abilities, yet I chose him to lead My people. Or Esther, an orphan girl who became a queen "for such a time as this" (Esther 4:14). Their pasts did not disqualify them; instead, I used their stories to shape their destinies.

You do not have to have it all figured out. Your destiny unfolds as you trust Me, as you take small steps of faith, even when fear whispers that you are not enough. But you *are* enough—not because of your strength, but because of Mine within you.

I am the Author of your story, and I am not finished writing. Every setback, every detour, even the broken chapters—I can weave them into a beautiful tapestry of redemption. Nothing is wasted in My hands. What the enemy meant for harm, I will turn for good (Genesis 50:20).

Do not compare your journey to others. Your destiny is not a competition; it is a calling. It is the unique imprint of My heart on your life. Whether it feels big or small, seen or unseen, it matters to Me.

So rise, beloved. Step into the fullness of who you are. You are called, chosen, and destined for greatness in Me. I am with you, guiding your steps, cheering you on, and reminding you every day:

You have a destiny, and it is beautiful.

With unwavering purpose,

Your Heavenly Father

"For I know the plans I have for you," declares the Lord, "plans to prosper you and not to harm you, plans to give you hope and a future."

JEREMIAH 29:11

A Final Letter For You

Beloved,

As you reach the end of these pages, know this is not the end of My message to you. In fact, it is only the beginning. My love for you is not confined to words on a page; it is alive, active, and eternal, written across the very fabric of your heart.

You are loved with a love that knows no boundaries, cherished beyond measure, and pursued with relentless grace. I see you fully—your beauty, your struggles, your hopes, and your fears. And in seeing you, I love you completely. There is nothing hidden from Me, yet nothing that could ever separate you from My love (Romans 8:38-39).

No matter where you have been or what you have faced, I have been with you through it all. My hands have held you in your sorrow, My whispers have called you in the silence, and My heart has celebrated your joys. I am not distant or far off; I am closer than your very breath.

So here is My love letter to you:

My beloved child,

I delight in you. You are precious to Me, and nothing you do can change that. I formed you with intention, crafted you with care, and breathed My life into you. You are not an accident; you are a masterpiece.

When you feel lost, I am your way. When you feel broken, I am your healer. When you feel unseen, I am the One who sees you, knows you, and calls you by name.

You are not defined by your past, your mistakes, or your fears. You are defined by My love, My grace, and My purpose for your life. I have plans for you—plans to prosper you, to give you hope, and a future filled with promise.

Rest in My love. Let it be the foundation beneath your feet, the song in your heart, and the peace within your soul. You are never alone, for I am with you always.

I love you with an everlasting love. I always have, and I always will.

With all My heart,

Your Heavenly Father

May these words echo in your heart long after you close this book. You are loved, cherished, pursued, and destined for a life filled with My presence. Hold this truth close, and never forget:

You are My beloved, forever and always.

An Invitation

Dear Friend,

As you have read these pages, I hope you have felt the tender whisper of God's love calling to your heart. Maybe you have been longing for something more—for a peace that lasts, a love that never fails, and a hope that anchors your soul. That longing is not an accident. It is the gentle pull of the One who created you, who knows you, and who loves you beyond measure.

If you do not yet know Jesus as your personal Lord and Savior, I want you to know this: His arms are open wide, and His heart beats with love for you. He came to earth, lived a perfect life, and gave His life on the cross so that you could be forgiven, redeemed, and brought into a relationship with God.

You do not have to clean yourself up or have all the answers. You simply have to come as you are. Jesus is not looking for perfection; He is looking for your heart.

Here is His invitation to you:

"Come to Me, all who are weary and burdened, and I will give you rest." (Matthew 11:28)

If you feel that tug on your heart, do not ignore it. This is your moment. He is calling you into a relationship, not a religion—into a love that is personal, real, and eternal.

You can begin this journey with a simple prayer, from your heart to His:

"Jesus, I need You. I believe You are the Son of God, that You died for my sins, and that You rose again. I confess my need for Your forgiveness. I surrender my heart to You. Be my Lord and Savior. Fill me with Your love, Your peace, and Your purpose. Thank You for loving me and for giving me new life. Amen."

If you prayed that prayer, heaven is rejoicing, and so am I. This is not the end; it is the beautiful beginning of a life with Jesus.

What's next?

- Find a Bible and start reading, beginning with the Gospel of John.

- Talk to God daily. Prayer is simply a conversation with the One who loves you most.

- Connect with a community of believers who can encourage you in your new faith.

You are loved. You are chosen. You are now part of God's family, and nothing will ever change that.

With love and joy, Your Friend in Christ,

Tonya

About the Author

About the Author

Tonya Kay McKinley is a passionate speaker, minister, and writer with a heart for empowering women to embrace their God-given identity. She holds a degree in Theology and has dedicated her life to helping others discover the transformative love of Christ.

Tonya makes her home in North Carolina, where she lives with her faithful and furry companion, Boulder. Whether she's walking scenic trails, diving into scripture, or sharing her message at women's events, she brings warmth, humor, and authenticity to everything she does.

As the founder of Hadassah Ministries, Tonya equips women to walk boldly in their calling as daughters of the King. Through her writing, she invites readers to explore their faith, face life's challenges with a TIARA attitude, and find their unique place in God's kingdom.

Other Works

"Stumbling Down the Road Less Traveled: A Devotional: Insights Into Life's Mishaps on the Road." Published February, 2008.

"Finding Your Love Story: Fall in Love with the One Who Loved Your First." Published August, 2021.

"Finding Your Love Story: A Bible Study: Fall in Love with the One Who Loved You First." Published August, 2021.

"A Princess Proclamation." Published January, 2024.

"A Prince's Pledge." Published January, 2024.

www.hadassah-ministries.org

*We would love to hear
from you, visit our web-
page by scanning the QR
code.*

A Final Word of Encouragement:

Beloved, never forget that you are seen, known, and deeply
loved. Your life is a beautiful story still being written by the
Author of love Himself. Lean into Him, trust His heart,
and walk boldly in the truth that you are cherished beyond
measure.

You are loved. You are chosen. You have a destiny.

www.ingramcontent.com/pod-product-compliance
Lightning Source LLC
Chambersburg PA
CBHW060545030426
42337CB00021B/4437